With Love, I Let Go

A JOURNEY BACK TO SELF

Angelita Byrd

Book Title: (With Love I Let Go A Journey Back to Self)

Author: (Angelita Byrd)

Preface

This book was born from the kind of pain that changes you. The kind of healing that demands you break open before you break free. With Love, I Let Go is not just a story— it's a reckoning, a reclaiming, and a return.

For far too long, I lived in spaces that asked me to shrink, sacrifice, and silence the deepest parts of myself. I gave love that wasn't reciprocated, loyalty that wasn't valued, and energy that drained my spirit. I held on—not because I didn't know better, but because I hadn't yet remembered who I was.

This journey back to self wasn't graceful or linear. It was messy. Raw. Sacred. There were days I doubted my strength, nights I mourned what I thought I couldn't live without, and moments I had to remind myself that survival wasn't the same as healing. And still—I kept going.

This book is for anyone who has ever lost themselves in someone else. For the ones who gave too much, stayed too long, or settled for less. It's for the strong ones—the silent warriors—who carry the weight of the world and still find the courage to choose themselves.

My hope is that these pages will meet you where you are and

gently lead you back home—to your truth, your worth, your peace.

Because letting go isn't a weakness. It's an act of love.

And coming back to yourself?

That's the bravest thing you'll ever do.

With love, Angelita Byrd

Acknowledgment

To all of my exes,

Thank you.

For the love you gave me—for as long or as little as it lasted.

For the joy and the pain.

For the lessons that broke me and the growth that built me.

You were a chapter in my story, not the ending.

And though some of those pages still sting, they shaped a woman who now loves herself more deeply than she ever thought possible.

Your absence became the space where I found my strength.

Your silence, the soundtrack to my healing.

And your betrayal, the spark that ignited my self-worth.

I don't carry bitterness—I carry wisdom.

I don't wish you harm—I wish myself peace.

Because of you, I learned how to return home to me.

With love, I let go.

— Angelita Byrd

Table of Contents

Chapter 1: 1

The Call I Shouldn't Have Answered.......... 1

Chapter 2: 7

Before the Storm.......... 7

Chapter 3: 13

The Moment I Knew 13

Chapter 4: 20

The Becoming 20

Chapter 5: 25

The Sacred Stillness 25

Chapter 6: 30

You're Too Late 30

Chapter 7: 37

I Will Not Shrink Again 37

Chapter 8: 42

I Am My Own Joy.......... 42

Chapter 9: 47

Chosen by Purpose 47

Chapter 10: 53

The Grace to Outgrow 53

Chapter 11: 58

Wholeness, Finally 58

Chapter 12: 63

Living in Overflow 63

Chapter 13: 70

I Am the Love I Was Looking For 70

Chapter 1:

The Call I Shouldn't Have Answered

I knew the number before it lit up on my phone.

I didn't need to see the name — my body recognized the energy before my eyes ever caught up.

It's strange how someone's vibration can still echo in your soul long after the love has gone quiet.

I stared at the screen.

I hesitated.

Then I answered.

It started with small talk — the kind you use to mask the real reason you're calling. The voice sounded familiar, but something in the tone was hollow, like a song you once loved that now plays out of tune.

We talked. Then we talked again.

Eventually, we agreed to meet in person — not to rekindle anything, not to fall back into old
flames, but just to I don't know. See if peace could find us.

Closure maybe. Friendship if the stars aligned.

But let me tell you something about intuition:

It never whispers without a reason. Mine was screaming the whole time.

Still, I made room. I opened the door.

I greeted a man I once would've sworn was my forever.

And the moment he walked in…

I felt everything in me tense. My heart sank.

My stomach turned.

My body, my spirit, my knowing — they all screamed the truth I didn't want to hear:

"This ain't it anymore."

He sat down. I listened. He talked. I nodded.

But I couldn't find that thread — that invisible line that once connected our souls.

Instead, I saw a man I no longer recognized.

The stories he told were dressed in delusion. His words lacked weight. His energy was off, heavy with denial, light on truth. He wore a smile that felt performative. Hollow. The kind you wear when you've practiced in the mirror too long.

And still, he claimed to love me.

He said I was the only one who ever truly challenged him. That no other woman pushed him to be more. That I was his standard.

But here's what I know now:

If love doesn't come with accountability, it isn't love.

If someone can sleep peacefully after wounding your spirit, that's not love — that's convenience.

And I… I am not a convenience.

I'm a force.

A healer.

A divine woman who knows her worth — even when her

heart still wants to believe the best in people.

So I sat there. Quiet but clear.

I let him speak. And then I spoke back — not from pain, but from clarity.

I told him the truth:

You'll spend the rest of your life looking for what you had in me.

Not because I was perfect. But because I showed up — heart first, soul open, crown unshaken.

And you let that go. Twice.

There was a time I would've begged you to rise. A time I would've fought your demons for you. But now? I've laid down the sword.

That was never my battle to fight.

This is how the healing began.

Not with fireworks. Not with tears.

But with a calm certainty that said:

"I love you. And I still have to let you go."

Because love isn't enough when peace is at stake.

Because some doors were meant to close.

And because I deserve more than someone who only realizes my value after I'm gone.

So I share this chapter, not to shame him — but to free myself.

This is not a love story. This is a liberation story.

With Love, I Reflect..

What emotions surfaced while reading this chapter?

Which part of the story felt most personal or familiar?

What truth am I ready to accept or release today?

Chapter 2:

Before the Storm

Before everything cracked, there was warmth. Before the silence, there was laughter.

Before I had to let go, there was a time when I held him with everything I had — arms, mind, heart, and prayer.

We didn't start in perfection, but we started in sincerity.

He came into my life like a gentle storm — a presence I couldn't ignore.

There was a fire in his voice, a charm in his walk, and a story in his eyes that made me want to listen longer than I should have.

And when we connected, it was more than attraction — it was familiar.

It was like meeting someone I'd known in another life.

We talked for hours. About everything. About nothing.

He made me laugh when I didn't even realize I needed joy.

And I gave him space he never knew he needed — space to just be.

Not perform. Not prove. Just… exist.

In the early days, it felt like we were building something sacred.

We shared dreams like secrets, planned futures without knowing how fragile they'd become.

We prayed together. Played together. Fell into rhythms that felt like music.

He wasn’t perfect, and neither was I.

But we showed up — raw, real, and ready. Or so I thought.

And then life began to happen.

Slowly, cracks began to form — little lies dressed as omissions. Inconsistencies explained with charm and distractions.

And me? I chose to believe the best.

Because I wanted to believe that love — real love — could weather anything.

I stood by him. Through losses, through setbacks, through things that would’ve broken others.

I carried his weight when he grew tired. Covered his shame with my silence.

Built him up while neglecting my own foundation.

Because I loved him. Deeply. Boldly. Fiercely.

The kind of love that doesn't walk away easily.

The kind of love that forgives before it even hears the apology.

But somewhere between our beginnings and the breakdown, I started losing pieces of myself.

The laughs became less frequent. The joy became strained.

And the respect — that sacred thread — began to fray.

Still, I stayed.

Not because I didn’t know better, but because I remembered

who he used to be.

I stayed for the man who showed up in the beginning.

For the version of him that could light up a room, speak life into strangers, and make me feel like the safest place on earth.

But that man became harder and harder to find.

And I became lonelier and lonelier beside someone I once couldn't live without.

I began to realize…

I wasn't in love with him anymore.

I was in love with the memory of us.

There's something heartbreaking about watching someone unravel — especially when

you've seen their brilliance.

I begged him to heal.

I fought for his freedom more than he ever fought for his own. And in doing so, I almost lost mine.

But make no mistake:

Ours was not all pain. There was beauty.

There were moments of magic I'll never forget.

He taught me that love can be raw and consuming.

That two people can want each other deeply and still not be ready.

That sometimes, love alone isn't enough to keep something

whole.

So I hold the past with tenderness — not regret.

Because even though it didn't end the way I hoped,

it taught me to never again shrink myself to save someone else. It taught me the cost of pouring from an empty cup.

And it taught me that sometimes the most loving thing you can do…is walk away.

With Love, I Reflect..

What emotions surfaced while reading this chapter?

Which part of the story felt most personal or familiar?

What truth am I ready to accept or release today?

Chapter 3:

The Moment I Knew

I do not chase peace

I create it inside myself.

And I honor what protects it. ❤

It wasn't one big betrayal.

It wasn't some loud explosion of truth or final straw that shattered everything at once. No, it was quieter than that.

Subtle. Sharp.

Final in its stillness.

It was the moment I looked at him — really looked at him — and realized… I didn't recognize the man in front of me anymore.

We were sitting across from each other — in a space that should have felt familiar. I had convinced myself we could at least find some kind of peace.

Maybe even laugh again, just as two people who once meant everything to each other.

But what sat in front of me wasn't a friend. It wasn't a man capable of loving me.

It wasn't someone safe for my soul.

He talked.

But it was all smoke.

Stories stitched together with lies. Excuses wrapped in charm.

Accountability nowhere to be found.

And as he rambled on — about life, about other women, about how no one "gets him" the

way I do — I felt a calm clarity begin to wash over me.

It wasn't rage.

It wasn't sadness.

It was something far more sacred: Relief.

That was the moment.

The exact second I knew — I was done.

Not in a petty way.

Not in a wounded way. But in a healed way.

I wasn't angry that he couldn't love me the way I deserved.

I was angry at myself for waiting so long to admit it.

He said he still loved me. That he always would.

That no one else challenged him, saw him, or stood beside him like I did.

But here's the thing:

Love is more than words. More than promises.

More than presence.

Love shows up.

Love grows up.

Love doesn't keep returning just to take more than it gives.

And there I was — sitting across from a man who once had my whole heart —

feeling like a stranger was trying to sell me a memory I no longer wanted.

My body had already known.

It had been trying to tell me for months.

The nausea. The exhaustion. The anxiety I felt just hearing his name.

But that day, my spirit caught up.

And something inside me finally whispered:

"Let it go. For real this time. You don't belong here anymore."

I didn't storm out. I didn't cry.

I didn't plead with him to do better.

I just sat back.

And let the silence between us speak what my words no longer needed to say:

This is the end.

Not out of bitterness.

But out of boundless self-love.

He didn't even notice the shift.

Didn't see the moment my heart packed its bags and walked out the door, because he was too busy rehearsing his charm for someone else.

And that told me everything I needed to know.

That was the moment.

The moment I stopped looking for signs.

Stopped waiting for him to change.

Stopped holding my breath hoping to feel whole again.

The moment I exhaled and whispered to myself:

"You made it. You're free."

With Love, I Reflect..

What emotions surfaced while reading this chapter?

Which part of the story felt most personal or familiar?

What truth am I ready to accept or release today?

Chapter 4:

The Becoming

Letting go is only the first step.

The real work begins in the silence that follows.

When the door finally closes… and all you're left with is you.

No more distractions.

No more rehearsed conversations.

No more waiting for the apology that never came.

Just you. Your heart. Your breath.

And the pieces of yourself you forgot how to hold.

In the days after I let go, I didn't bounce back.

I unraveled.

Quietly.

Beautifully. Painfully.

Not because I missed him — but because I had to mourn the version of myself that stayed too long.

I cried.

I slept more than I usually do. I lit candles.

I wrote letters I never sent.

And I sat in rooms filled with silence until that silence started to feel like a friend.

There's something sacred about starting over — not with a new person, but with yourself.

I started asking questions I hadn't asked in years:

What do I really want?

What makes me feel alive?

Who am I when I'm not saving, fixing, or over-giving?

The answers didn't come all at once.

They came in small ways:

In morning walks.

In songs that found me when I needed them most.

In the moments I said "no" without explaining.

In the long baths where I didn't rush to get out.

In the quiet pride of choosing peace over proving my worth.

I stopped performing.

I stopped apologizing for needing space.

I stopped waiting to be chosen and chose myself instead.

And slowly, the woman I used to be — the one I had tucked away beneath all the caretaking and compromise — started to return.

Not the same. Stronger.

Wiser.

Softer, but sharper. More discerning.

More mine.

Healing didn't look perfect.

Some days, I questioned everything.

Some nights, I missed the idea of him — not the man, but the memories. But even in that, I never wanted to go back.

Because I finally understood:

Peace > Passion that steals your peace.

I learned that I am allowed to want it all —

to be held, seen, heard, respected, and free.

And I stopped begging people to love me in ways they weren't taught to love themselves.

This season of healing became a season of becoming.

I became the woman who: sets boundaries without guilt protects her softness with fire. chooses solitude over shallow connections knows her worth even when no one else is clapping.

I look in the mirror now, and I don’t see a woman broken by heartbreak —

I see a woman rebuilt by truth.

And it’s not that I stopped loving him… It’s that I started loving me more.

That’s the true miracle of letting go:

It gives you back to yourself.

With Love, I Reflect..

What emotions surfaced while reading this chapter?

Which part of the story felt most personal or familiar?

What truth am I ready to accept or release today?

Chapter 5:

The Sacred Stillness

There was a time when silence scared me.

I used to fill every quiet moment with noise — conversations, distractions, tasks, people I had no business entertaining.

Anything to avoid being alone with myself.

Because solitude forces truth to rise. And truth?

It doesn't whisper.

It sits with you… stares you in the face… and dares you to stop pretending.

But something shifted when I let go. The noise fell away.

And for the first time in a long time, I didn't reach for anything.

I let myself feel the stillness — even when it was uncomfortable. I let myself sit with the ache, the questions, the grief, the quiet.

And what I discovered was this:

Solitude isn't punishment. It's purification.

In the quiet, I heard God more clearly. Not in thunder, but in whispers.

You are not forgotten.

You are not broken.

You are being brought back to yourself.

This is the healing before the harvest.

I realized that much of my exhaustion hadn't come from life

itself...but from fighting for people, relationships, and versions of me that no longer served my soul.

When you finally stand still, when you stop running from yourself—

you begin to see the difference between what's heavy and what's holy.

And I had been carrying so much… that wasn't mine.

Solitude became my sanctuary. No longer lonely — but full.

Full of clarity. Full of grace. Full of divine reminders of who I've always been beneath the

wounds.

I began waking up differently.

More grounded.

More aware.

More protective of my energy.

I stopped answering calls from people who only reached out when they needed something.

I stopped chasing closure from those who couldn't offer truth.

I stopped performing for love and started becoming a magnet for alignment.

Because when you truly reconnect with Spirit, you no longer beg to be seen. You are seen — by the One who matters most.

I found God again… not in a church pew, but in the hush of my breath during a sunrise walk.

In the way my heart beat slower when I stopped texting back.

In the tears that fell not from pain — but from freedom.

I found myself again… in the parts of me I had abandoned for the sake of being chosen.

This chapter of solitude has not been easy.

But it's been holy. It's been healing.

And most of all — it's been mine.

This is what spiritual alignment looks like:

Saying "no" without guilt.

Praying without pleading.

Releasing people without resentment.

Trusting divine timing more than temporary feelings.

Returning to yourself without apology.

I no longer fear the stillness. I honor it.

Because it's here — in the sacred silence — that I finally remembered who I am.

And who I've always been becoming.

With Love, I Reflect..

What emotions surfaced while reading this chapter?

Which part of the story felt most personal or familiar?

What truth am I ready to accept or release today?

Chapter 6:

You're Too Late

I am allowed to change.
To choose myself.
To begin again, with love. ♡

They always come back. Sometimes with flowers. Sometimes with apologies.

Sometimes with the same tired stories, dressed up in new intentions.

But when healing has rooted itself in your bones…

when you've done the soul work, cried the cleansing tears, reclaimed your peace — those "returns" hit differently.

They no longer pull you back.

They remind you just how far you've come.

It happened one quiet afternoon.

The kind of day where my spirit felt light and my thoughts didn't ache.

The message came through:

"Hey… I've been thinking about you."

I read it.

And for the first time in a long time, I didn't flinch.

No spark. No weight.

No war inside my heart.

Just a deep exhale — the kind that carries wisdom.

Because I knew exactly what it was.

It wasn't love.

It wasn't transformation.

It was the echo of a man finally realizing he lost access to something sacred.

Me.

They come back when they feel the absence of your light.

Not because they're ready to love you right —

but because your silence grew louder than their ego.

They remember the warmth. The patience.

The way you showed up when no one else did.

But what they forget…is the cost you paid for staying.

They remember how you made them feel. But they never truly saw what you needed.

And by the time they realize it — you've already become the version of yourself who no

longer waits.

I didn't respond right away.

Not because I was angry.

But because I didn't owe the old version of him — or the old version of me — anything.

I used to crave those messages.

Used to hope they'd come with clarity. With changed hearts. With redemption.

But healing teaches you this:

Not everyone deserves to witness who you become after they broke you.

Forgiveness doesn't mean reunion. Closure doesn't require conversation.

And just because someone wants to come back, doesn't mean they've earned the right to stand beside the woman you've evolved into.

So, when he said he still loved me…

I believed him.

But love isn't the question anymore.

Alignment is. Consistency is. Character is.

And he didn't bring any of those with him.

So I wished him well — in my heart, not in my inbox.

And I got back to living a life he will only ever see from a distance.

Because once you've healed…

Once you've built peace that doesn't require performance…

You don't let old chaos rent space in your new sanctuary.

To every woman reading this:

When they try to return, remember who you became. Remember the nights you held yourself.

The mornings you chose yourself. The boundaries you bled to build.

You are not obligated to reopen doors you've spiritually sealed.

Let them knock. Let them wonder. Let them miss you.

But do not let them back in just because they're finally looking for what they weren't ready to honor.

You are not the same woman they left behind. And they are too late.

With Love, I Reflect..

What emotions surfaced while reading this chapter?

Which part of the story felt most personal or familiar?

What truth am I ready to accept or release today?

Chapter 7:

I Will Not Shrink Again

There was a time when I made myself smaller so love could feel bigger.

A time when I bent, folded, and softened myself into shapes just to fit into spaces that weren't designed to hold me.

A time when I confused tolerance with love and attachment with worth.

But those days are gone.

Buried with the version of me who begged for crumbs while setting a full table for someone who never learned how to eat with gratitude.

I will not shrink again.

I remember how it felt — that quiet erosion.

The slow, daily compromise of my voice, my needs, my joy.

Not all at once.

But inch by inch.

I didn't even notice I was disappearing.

I just wanted to be enough. To be chosen.

To be loved in return for all the love I gave.

So I said "yes" when I meant "no." Laughed when I wanted to cry.

Stayed when I wanted to walk away.

Held my breath in rooms where my spirit couldn't breathe.

And I told myself I was being patient when really, I was abandoning myself.

Healing taught me something sacred:

Love that requires your silence is not love. Connection that demands your dimming is not divine. And worth is not earned — it is remembered.

So I started remembering.

I remembered that I am not too much.

That I don't need to shrink to be digestible.

That I was never designed to be someone's almost, maybe, or sometimes.

I am a full experience.

A storm and a sanctuary.

A force that deserves to be met — not managed.

There's power in standing tall in your truth.

Power in no longer chasing approval or begging to be kept.

Power in realizing that being alone is never as painful as being unseen while standing next to someone.

I now protect my peace like it's oxygen.

I don't argue to prove my value. I don't beg to be understood.

And I no longer contort myself into someone else's fantasy of who I should be.

Because the right people won't ask you to shrink.

They won't flinch at your fire or recoil from your softness.

They'll honor your fullness — not fear it.

So this is my declaration:

I will not shrink again.

Not to make someone else feel more secure. Not to maintain access to shallow connection. Not to keep peace that costs me myself.

I am not negotiable.

My voice is not disposable.

And my light will not be dimmed for anyone who can't handle the brightness.

To every woman who has ever made herself smaller to feel loved:

I see you.

I know you.

But you don't have to do that anymore.

Stand tall. Speak fully.

Love boldly — especially yourself.

And walk away from anything that asks you to be less than who you were created to be.

You are not too much.

You were always just enough for the right heart.

With Love, I Reflect..

What emotions surfaced while reading this chapter?

Which part of the story felt most personal or familiar?

What truth am I ready to accept or release today?

Chapter 8:

I Am My Own Joy

There was a time I thought love would complete me.

I bought into the story — that romantic connection was the prize. That being chosen was the ultimate validation.

That partnership meant I had finally arrived.

But what I've come to learn is this:

Happiness is not housed in another person.

It's rooted in the home you build within yourself.

When I walked away from that relationship, I didn't just grieve him.

I grieved the idea that love was the only path to wholeness.

I had to confront the silence that followed — the evenings with no calls, no "how was your day," no hand to hold.

And in that silence…

I began to hear my own laughter again. Feel my own rhythm.

Reclaim the beauty of my own company.

There is so much life outside of romantic love. There is depth.

There is wonder.

There is you — unfiltered, uninterrupted, and fully alive.

I started asking myself new questions:

What brings me joy that isn't dependent on someone else's presence?

What dreams have I postponed while waiting for "us" to happen?

Who am I when no one is watching — and would I still choose that version of me?

The answers came slowly, like sunrise over still water.

I found joy in simple things:

Cooking barefoot to my favorite playlist. Long walks with no destination.

Books that made me weep.

Sunlight dancing on my skin without needing to be seen by anyone else.

I found freedom in choosing myself — day after day — and discovering that it was more than enough.

Somewhere along the way, we're taught that a woman without a man must be missing something.

That success, beauty, even joy — mean less without a ring, a partner, a love story wrapped in romance.

But here's what I know now:

Your life doesn't begin when you are loved by another.

It begins when you learn to love yourself with the same tenderness you've given away.

Romantic love is beautiful. But it is not everything.

And sometimes, we have to lose the fairytale to find the truth:

That you can be happy, whole, and wildly fulfilled without anyone else writing your story.

I've learned how to date myself.

To spoil myself.

To take myself out and make no apologies for enjoying it.

To buy the flowers.

To book the trip.

To celebrate my wins without waiting for someone to clap for me.

And in doing so, I've become someone I genuinely enjoy being around.

I no longer crave a relationship to escape loneliness. I crave alignment, not attachment.

Wholeness, not healing projects.

And from this space of overflow — not emptiness — I can love others without losing myself.

So if you're in the space between heartbreak and healing…

If you're wondering whether joy still exists without romance…

Let me reassure you:

It does.

And when you stop chasing love, you start becoming it.

You are the love you've been waiting for. And there is nothing more beautiful than a woman who has learned to keep herself full.

With Love, I Reflect..

What emotions surfaced while reading this chapter?

Which part of the story felt most personal or familiar?

What truth am I ready to accept or release today?

Chapter 9:

Chosen by Purpose

Every time I choose healing over habit,

I come home to myself again. ♡

There comes a moment — often after the heartbreak, after the letting go, after the long nights of questioning everything — when the voice of purpose becomes louder than the longing for partnership.

That moment found me. And I finally listened.

Because the truth is…

I wasn't created just to be someone's "better half."

I wasn't born solely to be a partner, a placeholder, or someone's version of home.

I was born for impact.

For too long, I waited to "arrive" in life with someone.

As if my joy, my success, my legacy only counted if it was shared in tandem. But healing taught me:

Your calling doesn't wait for you to be coupled. Your purpose doesn't require permission.

And the destiny on your life isn't dependent on anyone walking beside you.

I used to put dreams on hold, thinking love would come first, and then I'd begin. But now I realize…

My purpose was the love story I was always meant to write.

I began to pour into it — not halfway, not conditionally, but fully.

I started the business. Told the story.

Launched the project. Shared the message.

Stood on the stages I once felt too broken to stand on.

And with each bold step forward, I felt more alive than any romantic connection had ever made me feel.

Because when you step into alignment —when you stop asking for permission to shine —you find a power that partnership alone can't give you.

You find you.

Purpose became my partner. My daily companion.

My driving force.

The reason I get up even when no one is clapping.

The fire that keeps me lit even when the nights feel long.

And it's not that I don't desire love — I do.

But I will never again pause my purpose waiting for partnership to catch up.

I will never shrink my mission to fit someone else's comfort zone.

I will never dim my voice because someone isn't ready to hear the truth it carries.

And I will never put down my crown just to be held by someone who doesn't know how to handle a Queen.

To every woman wondering if walking alone means walking empty:

You are not alone.

You are chosen — by God, by destiny, by something greater

than your past.

And that call on your life?

It won't wait for love to feel convenient.

You were meant to build, to lead,

to liberate,

to rise — whether or not someone is rising beside you.

Let them say you're "too focused." Let them say you're "doing too much." Let them call it intimidating.

But while they talk, you'll be out here changing lives.

Healing bloodlines. Breaking cycles.

Becoming the woman you prayed to become when your heart was still healing.

You're not behind.

You're not hard to love.

You're just deeply aligned.

And the right love?

If and when it comes…

Will honor the purpose that came first.

With Love, I Reflect..

What emotions surfaced while reading this chapter?

Which part of the story felt most personal or familiar?

What truth am I ready to accept or release today?

Chapter 10:

The Grace to Outgrow

There's a bittersweet kind of freedom in outgrowing someone you once saw forever with.

A quiet release that doesn't come with fireworks or final arguments — just peace. A knowing.

A whisper from your soul that says:

"You're not angry anymore…

You're just done evolving in their direction."

That's how I knew I had outgrown them.

Not because I stopped loving.

But because I stopped shrinking to stay connected.

There was a time I would've gone to war for their potential.

A time I praised them in public, covered them in prayer in private, and stood by them in

ways they didn't even stand by themselves.

I saw their light.

I held space for their becoming.

I believed — deeply — that love, patience, and support would be enough.

But then came the day I looked up and realized:

I was doing all the growing…

and all the giving.

They stayed the same.

Comfortable in the version of me who needed less, asked for less, and didn't yet know how much she was worth.

Growth is a gentle separation.

It doesn't always happen with slammed doors.

Sometimes it happens in the stillness… in the conversations that no longer land… in the laughter that feels forced… in the text messages that go unread because you no longer have the energy to explain who you've become.

And the truth is:

We outgrow people not because they're bad —

but because we've simply outlived the chapter they were written in.

That doesn't erase the good. It doesn't undo the love.

It just means… it's time.

I used to fear this kind of outgrowing.

I thought it meant I was being ungrateful, or disloyal, or too ambitious. I worried people would say I changed — and they did.

But now I realize:

You're supposed to change. That's the point of healing.

That's the reward of choosing yourself after years of emotional self-abandonment.

If your growth doesn't challenge your circle, you're probably still hiding parts of yourself.

So yes, I still smile when I think of the good times. I still wish them well.

I still remember how deeply I once believed they were part of my forever.

But I don't reach back.

Not because I'm bitter — but because I've been better since letting go.

I needed those relationships to teach me who I was.

But I needed to release them to become who I'm meant to be.

To every woman reading this who's outgrowing the familiar:

You're not wrong. You're not selfish. You're evolving.

And not everyone is meant to go where your healed self is headed.

You don't have to make it ugly to make it final.

You don't have to make a scene to make a decision.

You just have to love yourself enough to move in the direction of your expansion.

Peacefully. Powerfully.

And without apology.

With Love, I Reflect..

What emotions surfaced while reading this chapter?

Which part of the story felt most personal or familiar?

What truth am I ready to accept or release today?

Chapter 11:

Wholeness, Finally

There's a moment after the storms… after the unraveling, after the aching, after the silence has settled and your soul no longer flinches at the thought of the past…when you look in the mirror and quietly, deeply know:

"I'm whole."

Not perfect.

Not without scars.

Not above feeling — but whole.

Rooted.

Calm.

Unapologetically at home in your own skin.

I didn't arrive at wholeness all at once.

It didn't come in the form of a new relationship, or a breakthrough text, or some dramatic
ending that made everything make sense.

No… it came softly.

It came the day I stopped replaying conversations in my head.

The moment I no longer felt the urge to prove my worth to anyone who couldn't see it.

It came in the morning I woke up and didn't think about him first.

In the joy that met me without needing to be triggered by someone else's presence.

Wholeness isn't loud.

It doesn't scream for attention.

It just is — steady, sacred, still.

I began to feel it in the smallest things:

The way I poured my coffee and smiled for no reason.

The way I danced alone in my kitchen — not for an audience, but for me.

The way I said "no" without guilt and "yes" without fear.

The way my peace became non-negotiable.

I no longer needed someone to complete me.

Because I was no longer walking around with pieces of myself missing.

I found those pieces in every hard decision. Every tear I wiped alone.

Every time I said, "This hurts, but I'm still choosing me."

The beauty of wholeness is this:

You're no longer waiting to be saved. You've become your own rescue.

You hold space for your own joy.

You wipe your own tears without resentment. You set the standard.

You write the story.

And when love shows up — if it does — it'll be met by someone who is already full.

Already grounded.

Already clear on who she is.

Because wholeness changes how you love — and how you allow yourself to be loved.

I used to think wholeness meant "I don't need anyone."

Now I understand:

Wholeness means I know I'm enough — whether I'm walking alone or hand in hand with

someone who sees me.

So here I am.

Not waiting. Not wounded.

Not wondering if I'll ever be okay again.

I am okay.

I am whole.

And I am so proud of the woman I became after it all fell apart.

To every woman still healing:

Wholeness is coming.

And when it arrives, it won't need to announce itself.

You'll just feel it — in your breath, in your bones, in your boundaries, in your joy.

And you'll know:

You finally made it back to yourself

.

With Love, I Reflect..

What emotions surfaced while reading this chapter?

Which part of the story felt most personal or familiar?

What truth am I ready to accept or release today?

Chapter 12:

Living in Overflow

The woman I'm becoming
was worth everything I had to let go. ♡

There is a moment after the healing after the lessons, after the release, after the rising when something unfamiliar but beautiful begins to happen:

You stop surviving.

And you start overflowing.

The love that once felt distant —you become it.

The joy you searched for in others —you generate it.

The strength you thought you had to earn you now embody.

Because when you've done the inner work, when you've cleared the clutter of confusion, and reconnected with your purpose, you no longer operate from lack.

You live from abundance.

Overflow feels different.

It's not loud.

It doesn't demand applause.

It's a quiet confidence.

A rooted joy.

It's waking up with clarity.

Walking into rooms without shrinking.

Showing up in love, in work, in purpose — full, not depleted.

You're no longer loving to be validated. You're loving because love flows through you. You're no longer creating to prove something.

You're creating because it's your divine language. You're

no longer leading to be seen.

You're leading because you've become light — and light doesn't ask permission to shine.

People can feel it. The shift.

The softness. The fire.

They don't know the tears you cried to get here.

The nights you doubted yourself.

The boundaries you had to build with trembling hands.

But you know.

And that's what makes this season of overflow so sacred.

You're no longer the woman begging for reciprocity. You're the woman choosing alignment.

You're the woman creating impact from a healed space. You're the woman saying:

"I don't just want peace… I am peace. I don't just want love… I am love."

And when you become what you once chased,

you stop settling for anything that doesn't honor who you've become.

Overflow looks like:

Saying yes to things that light your soul on fire.

Creating without over-explaining.

Loving without losing yourself.

Being soft and powerful at the same time.

Giving — not from obligation, but from overflow.

You're not afraid to pour into others now, because you've made pouring into yourself a daily practice.

This isn't the same woman who stayed too long.

This isn't the woman who watered dead things and called it love.

This is the woman who knows her power… and no longer apologizes for using it.

She leads with wisdom. She creates with purpose. She loves with discernment.

She gives from abundance, not emptiness.

And everything she touches —from business to relationships to legacy —bears the fingerprints of someone who's no longer trying to be enough…

because she already is.

To every woman rising:

You were never meant to just heal. You were meant to live in overflow.

To give, not from depletion — but from divine fullness.

Let this be your reminder:

You are not rebuilding just to return to who you were.

You are evolving into who you were always meant to be.

And that woman? She doesn't chase. She attracts.

She doesn't beg. She becomes.

She doesn’t compete.

She creates.

From joy. From clarity.

From overflow.

With Love, I Reflect..

What emotions surfaced while reading this chapter?

Which part of the story felt most personal or familiar?

What truth am I ready to accept or release today?

Chapter 13:

I Am the Love I Was Looking For

There's no heartbreak in this ending.

No regret. No anger.

Just a calm knowing that I found something far more powerful than closure.

I found me.

Whole. Healed. Here.

Now.

No longer reaching outside of myself for love.

No longer shrinking for spaces I've outgrown.

No longer explaining softness to people committed to misunderstanding it.

This is not a return. This is a rebirth.

Everything I once begged for —

To be seen. To be chosen. To be valued. To be safe…

I have become it.

I am the love I was looking for.

I am the warmth.

I am the protector.

I am the safe space. I am the standard.

I am the answered prayer I once sent up for someone else.

Let this be the final word —not just to the people I've released, but to the woman I used to be:

You were always worthy. Even before the healing.

Even when you stayed too long. Even when your voice

trembled.

Even when you forgot your own power.

I forgive you. I thank you.

I carry you forward — wiser, stronger, softer.

This is my declaration now:

- I choose me — first, fully, finally.
- I no longer perform for love — I attract it in its purest form.
- I create space for joy, purpose, softness, and pleasure — without guilt.
- I lead with integrity and walk in rooms like I belong, because I do.
- I release all that was never meant to stay and honor all that helped me grow.
- I am no longer waiting to be chosen — I am the chosen one.
- I don't just survive anymore — I thrive.
- I don't chase — I align.
- I don't break — I evolve.

So let them wonder how I'm glowing without them.

Let them question how I healed without closure.

Let them realize, too late, what they once had access to.

Because this woman right here?

She's done doubting herself.

She's living in full bloom — watered by her own hands, lit by her own fire, anchored in her own love.

With love, I let go…and with love,

I return to myself—the greatest love of all.

With Love, I Reflect..

What emotions surfaced while reading this chapter?

Which part of the story felt most personal or familiar?

What truth am I ready to accept or release today?

Now that you've made it through every page,
I want you to pause.
Drop your shoulders.
Lift your head.
Take a deep breath.
Exhale.
Let it all go.

Let go of what they said.
Let go of who they wanted you to be.
Let go of the weight you were never meant to carry.
Let go of the shame, the guilt, the grief, the fear.

You've traveled through memories and truths, through heartbreak and healing.
You've stared your pain in the face and chose not to run.
And that, beloved, is bravery. That is love. That is freedom.

So before you close this book, know this:
You are no longer who you were when you began this journey.
You are softer but stronger.
Wiser and more rooted.
You are walking in truth.

And when the world tries to pull you back into old habits, whisper to yourself:
"With love, I let go."

This isn't the end—
It's a sacred beginning.
Your journey back to self continues.

With all my heart, ♡
Angelita Byrd

The End

But your journey… is just beginning.

To the Woman Still Healing…

You don't have to have it all figured out.

You don't have to be fully

"over it" to begin again.

Healing is not a destination—

it's a sacred remembering of who you are beneath the wounds.

If you still cry sometimes…

If you still miss them…

If some days feel heavier than others—

You're not failing.

You're healing.

There is no shame in having a soft heart in a hard world.

No weakness in choosing peace over performance.

And no timeline for how long it "should" take.

Go at your own pace.

Please know that you are not alone on this journey.

Every page of this book was written with you in mind—

with love, from one woman who's been through it, to another who's still walking it.

Keep going. With grace, with softness, with fire.

You are not broken, beloved.

You are becoming.

With all my heart,

Angelita Byrd

🍪 And when you're ready…

The next part of this journey lives inside A Girl Named Bitter—

A story about the ache beneath the armor, the voice behind the silence, and the fire it takes to turn pain into poetry.

Because some scars don't just heal… they speak.

Coming soon.

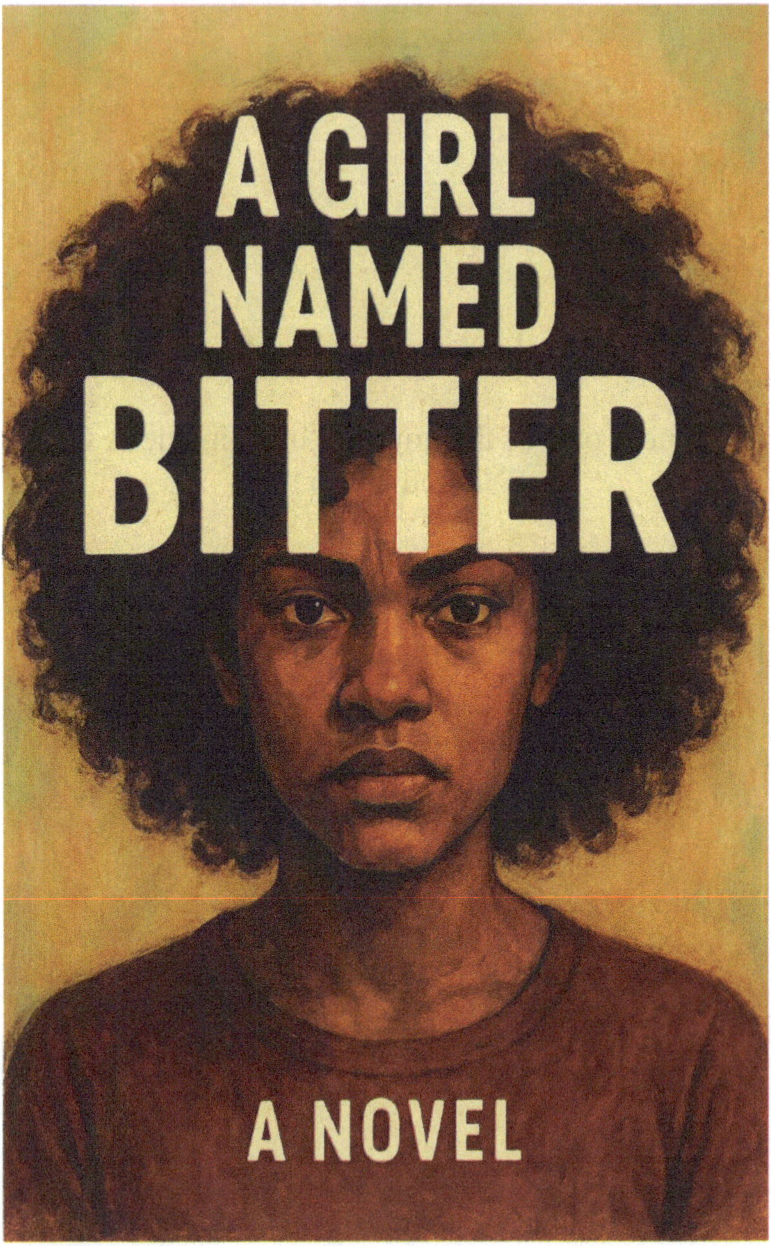
A GIRL
NAMED
BITTER
A NOVEL

Meet the Author
With Love,
I Let Go
A JOURNEY BACK TO SELF
by Angelita Byrd

About the Author

Angelita Byrd is a writer, truth-seeker, and healing voice for those on the path to emotional freedom. Through raw honesty and soulful reflection, she helps women release the pain of their past and return home to themselves.

With Love, I Let Go is her love letter to every woman who has ever lost herself while trying to hold on to someone else. With grace and grit, Angelita reminds us that letting go isn't giving up—it's giving up—it"s choosing yourself.

This book was born from a deeply personal experience—a season in her life when she had to choose healing over holding on. That journey became the inspiration behind every truth shared within these pages.

With Love I Let Go – A Journey Back to Self by Angelita Byrd

Join the Movement:

With Love I Let Go

Instagram:

@withloveiletgo

Website:

www.WithLoveILetGo.com

Facebook Community:

With Love I Let Go

Invite a friend to begin this healing journey too.

Made in the USA
Coppell, TX
25 March 2026

74083031R00056